Where do babies come from?

Invader

A note to parents

It is natural for children to ask questions. They are always eager to know about pregnancy, birth and the difference between boys and girls.
Sometimes, parents find it hard to answer these questions in a straightforward way. To explain to a young child how a new life is created can be difficult.

This book aims to help children to understand a little about sex, and what happens from the moment a baby is conceived to its birth.

Many children have been shown this book to test their reaction, and the diagrams and colour illustrations have proved to be very successful.

Introduction

Every living thing starts by being small. A giant tree was once a tiny sapling. A cow starts life as a calf, a pig as a piglet, and a hen as a chick. Every grown up person begins life as a baby.

It is because there are men and women that it is possible to make babies. Men and women are grown up boys and girls.

Let us find out the difference between boys and girls.

How are girls made?

A girl has a small opening at the base of her body, between her legs. Inside the opening are two little holes. The first hole is the one where the wee-wee (urine) comes out when a girl goes to the toilet. Behind this hole there is another, which is the entrance to a narrow passage called the **vagina.**

The illustration on the next page shows how the inside of this part of a girl's body looks.

The narrow passage, or vagina, leads to the **uterus**. The uterus is also known as the womb. It is the baby's first home, where it starts to grow and develop.
We will learn more about that in a moment.

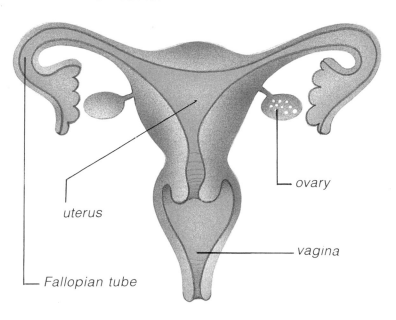

ovary

uterus

vagina

Fallopian tube

On each side of the uterus there are two thin tubes which open out at the ends: they are called the **Fallopian tubes**. Near the end of each Fallopian tube is an **ovary**. It is an oval shape.

Tiny **eggs** grow inside the ovaries. Every month, one of the ovaries produces a single egg.
All the sexual organs you can see in the picture – the vagina, the Fallopian tubes, the uterus and the ovaries – are the parts of a girl that will be used to make babies when she is grown up.
These parts of the body are known as the **female sexual organs**.

How are boys made?

Boys have sexual organs as well. But, unlike girls, these organs are not found inside the body.
At the base of their bodies, boys have a **penis**. This is sometimes called a willy, but its proper name is a penis.

Urine comes out of the penis when a boy goes to the toilet. The illustration on the next page shows how the inside of a penis looks.

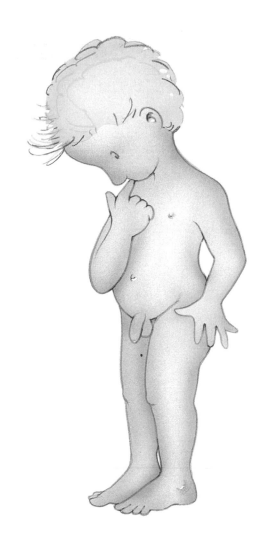

At the base of the penis there is a sack of skin, called the **scrotum** which contains two little balls. These are the **testicles**. A thin tube, called the **sperm duct**, leads from each testicle to the penis.

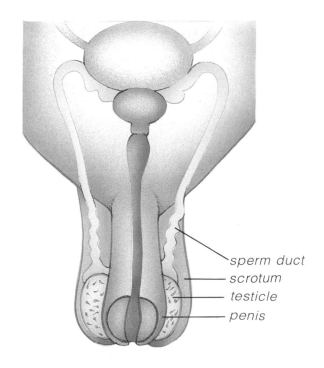

sperm duct
scrotum
testicle
penis

The sexual organs you can see in the picture – the penis, the scrotum, the testicles and the sperm ducts – are the parts of a boy that will be used to make babies when he is grown up. These parts of the body are known as the **male sexual organs**.

The little girl grows up

As a little girl grows older, her body changes. At about eleven years old her breasts begin to grow and hair starts to grow around her vagina. This hair helps to protect the vagina from dust and sweat. Hair also grows under the armpits.

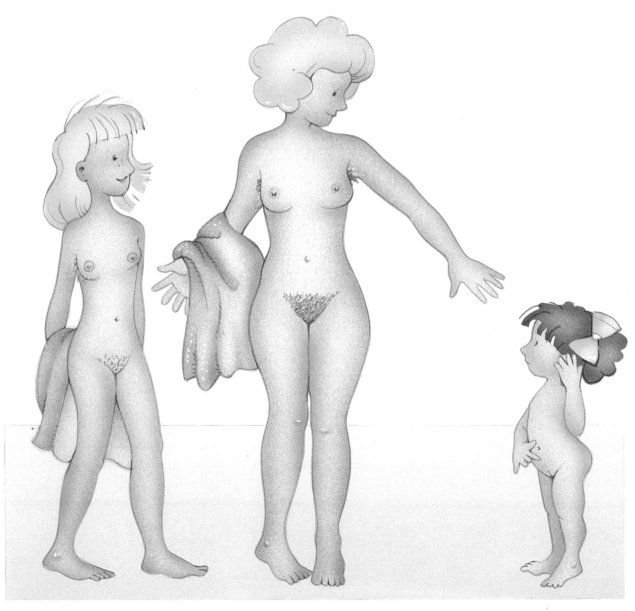

The changes do not only take place on the outside: other things happen inside her body.

The eggs in the ovaries ripen. Each month, a single egg leaves one of the ovaries and goes into a Fallopian tube: this is called **ovulation.** The egg slides gently down the tube towards the uterus.

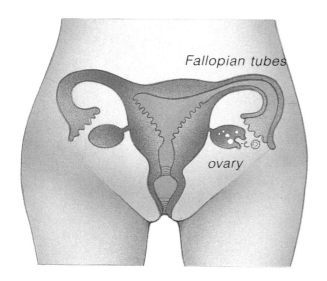

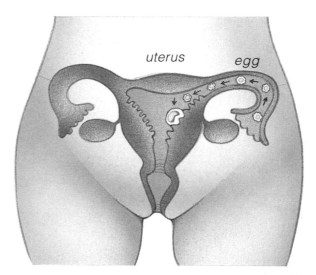

The little boy grows up

Boys also change as they grow older. At about thirteen years old, a boy's penis, scrotum and testicles become bigger. Hair appears at the base of the body, around the penis and under the arms. At the same time, the muscles in a boy's body start to develop and his voice deepens.

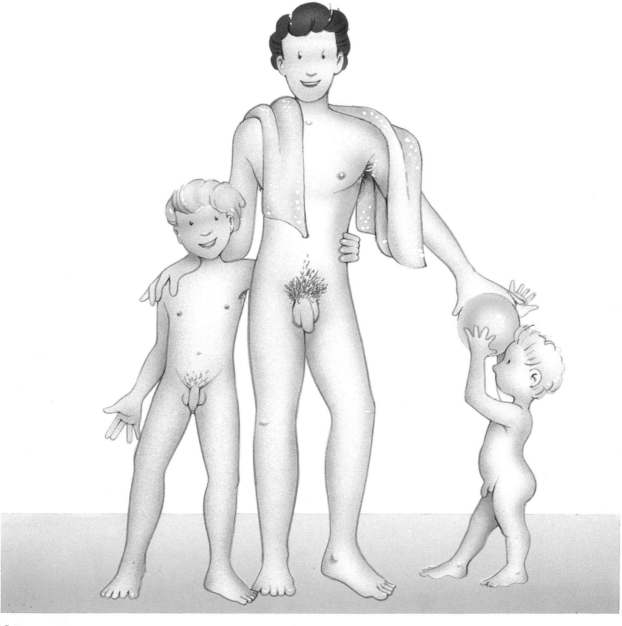

Later, hair starts to grow on other parts of the body, such as the chin and chest.

egg

sperm

At this time, a boy's testicles start to produce millions of **sperm.** Sperm are minute, much smaller than the eggs inside a girl's ovaries.

Sperm will not develop unless they are kept at a cool temperature and this is why the pouch (the scrotum) containing the testicles, is outside the body.

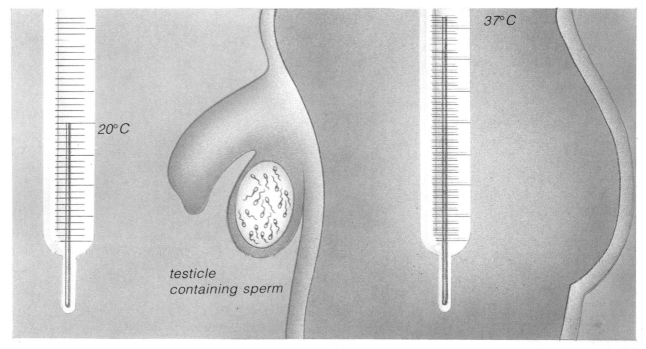

20°C

37°C

testicle containing sperm

Why do boys have sperm and girls have eggs?

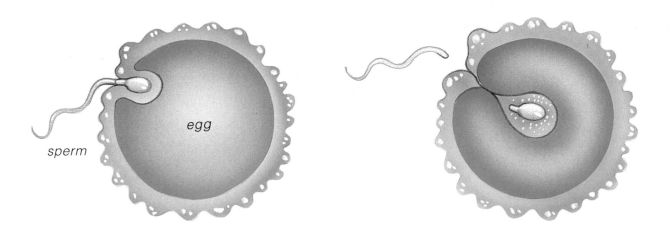

sperm

egg

When the sperm from a boy meet an egg from a girl, a small miracle happens: just one of the hundreds of sperm is allowed to wriggle its way inside the egg.

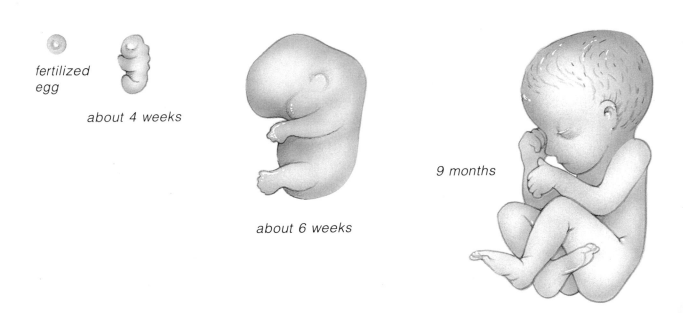

fertilized egg

about 4 weeks

about 6 weeks

9 months

The sperm and the egg join together, just as two drops of water form a new drop when they meet. This is the beginning of a baby.

How does the sperm find the egg?

Boys and girls grow into men and women. When a man and a woman love each other, they want to get as close to each other as they can. Boys and girls like to be kissed and cuddled by the people they love, and it is exactly the same for adults.

When a man and woman love each other, they want to hug and kiss, and sleep together. When they are in bed, they go on hugging and kissing.

The man's penis becomes longer and harder, and the woman's vagina becomes moist.

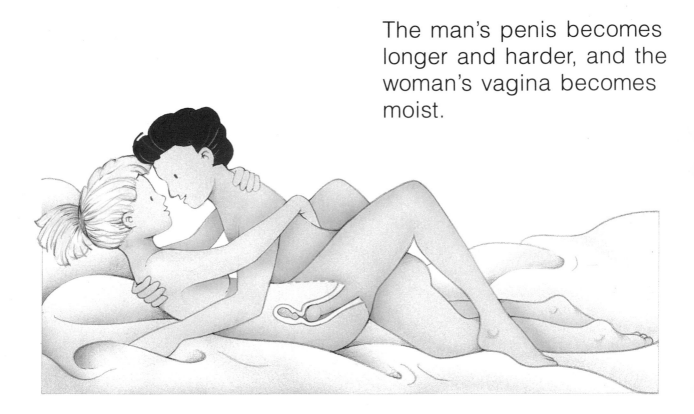

When this happens, the penis slides easily into the woman's vagina. It feels very nice for both the man and the woman.

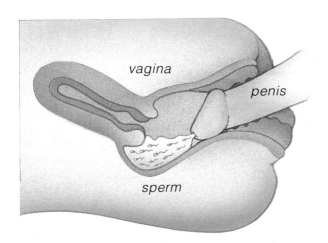

After a while, some liquid comes out of the end of the man's penis.

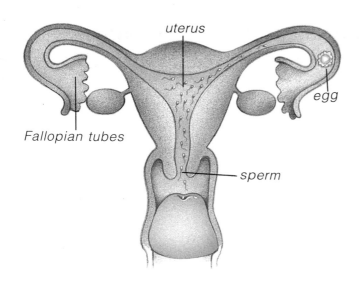

This liquid is called **semen** and it contains millions of sperm which have come from the testicles.
The sperm are too small for anyone to see, but each one has a head and a long tail, like a tadpole. They move along by wriggling their tails.

In this way, the sperm swim up the woman's vagina and into the uterus. They swim along the Fallopian tubes until they reach an egg.

Of the millions of sperm that came from the penis, only a few hundred will reach the egg and only one of them will be able to wriggle its way inside it.

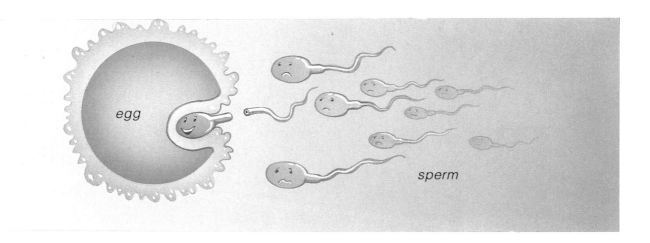

When the sperm and the egg join together, they make one cell. The moment when they join is called **fertilization.**

Fertilization normally takes place in a Fallopian tube. Several hours after fertilization has taken place, the cell divides; first into two cells, then four, eight, sixteen, and so on.

The ball of dividing cells moves down the Fallopian tube towards the uterus.
The cells will eventually become a boy or a girl depending on the sperm that fertilized the egg.
For a short while, the dividing cells look like a small, round ball. But it does not take long for the ball to grow and change shape.

The baby's first home

A few days after fertilization, the ball of cells reaches the uterus. It attaches itself to the uterus lining. It stays there for nine months while it grows into a baby.
The heart and brain develop, then the head, body, arms, legs, tiny fingers and toes begin to form.

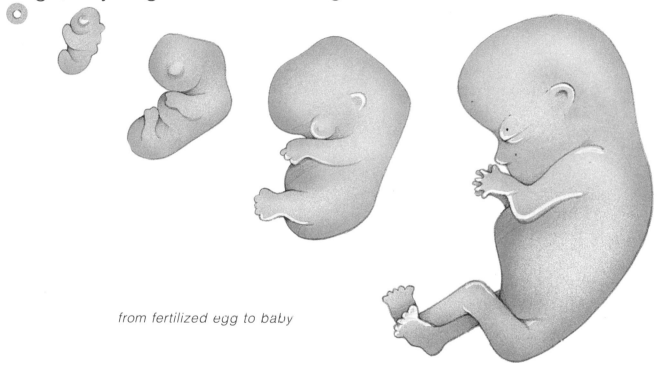

from fertilized egg to baby

But, just like boys and girls, the baby needs food in order to grow. A thin tube, called the **umbilical cord**, joins the baby to the lining of its mother's uterus. A **placenta** develops where the umbilical cord meets the uterus. The placenta is full of veins of blood containing food for the baby. The food is taken to the baby along the umbilical cord.

While it is in its mother's uterus, the baby floats in a bag of liquid. This liquid is called **amniotic fluid**. It keeps the baby warm and protects it from knocks and bumps. Because the baby is surrounded by fluid, it cannot breathe in oxygen through its nose or mouth. However, the baby receives oxygen from its mother through the umbilical cord.

Below is a picture showing a baby in its mother's uterus at 16 weeks old.

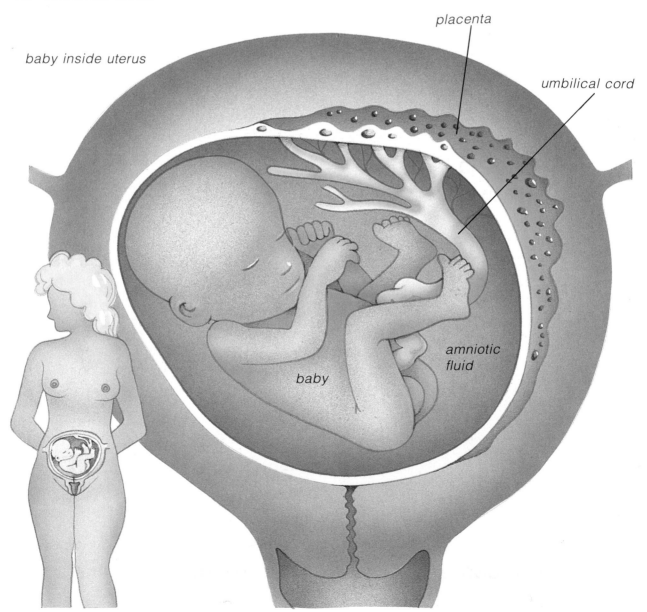

baby inside uterus

placenta

umbilical cord

amniotic fluid

baby

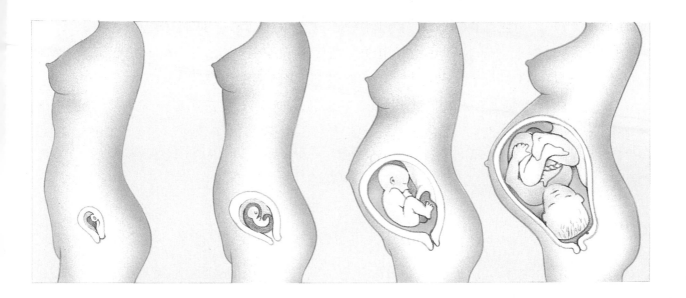

The baby grows bigger every day, and the uterus and the mother's tummy grow bigger as well. The uterus is like elastic, which stretches so that the baby has enough space to move around as it grows. If you put your hand on the stomach of a pregnant woman (a woman who is going to have a baby) you can sometimes feel the baby moving.

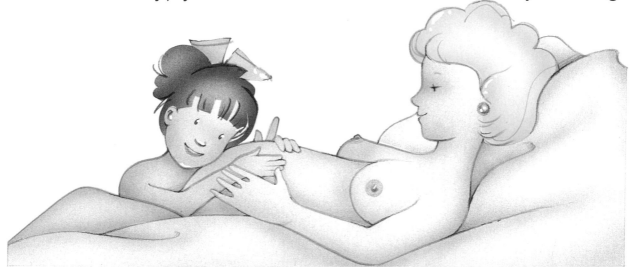

After nine months, the baby has grown so much that it does not have to be protected by its mother's body any more, and it can live in the outside world. Now is the time for the baby to be born.

How does a baby come out of its mother's tummy?

When it has been in its mother's uterus for nine months, the baby is ready to leave its first home.

The mother's body helps the baby on its way. The uterus squeezes and pushes the baby towards the vagina. This squeezing starts gently at first, but then it becomes stronger and the mother feels some pain. Now she knows her baby is ready to be born.

Most babies are born in hospital, so the mother and father go to one nearby. The mother is taken to the **maternity ward**, which is the part of a hospital reserved for **births**.

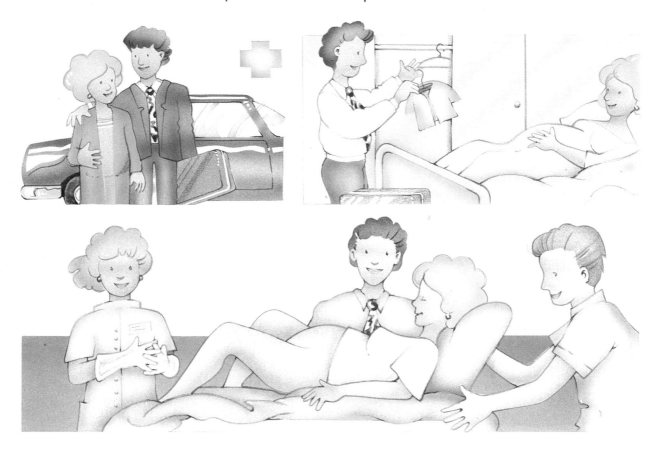

If a mother wants to give birth at home, a doctor and **midwife** visit her at her house. A midwife is a nurse who is specially trained to help mothers when babies are born.

All this time, the uterus continues to squeeze and push the baby towards the vagina. The vagina stretches when the baby passes through it. This part is hard work for the mother, who has to use her muscles to help her baby move down the vagina.

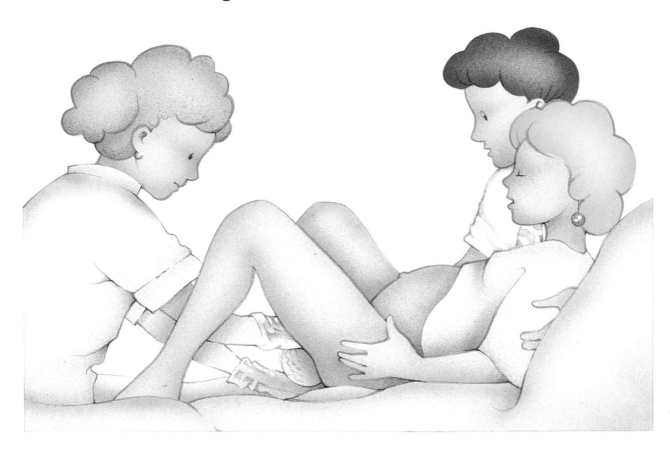

The baby's head is usually the first part to come out of the vagina, followed by its shoulders, its body and, finally, its legs.

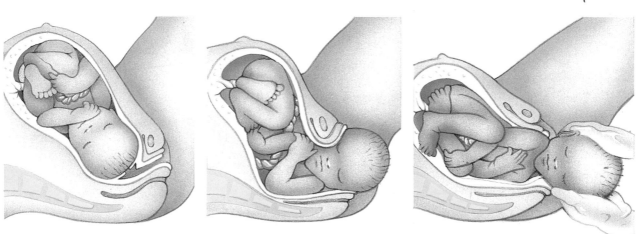

When the baby takes its first breath, it usually starts to cry – and no wonder! It has had a hard journey and it has left the warmth and comfort of its mother's body and found itself in a cold, bright world.

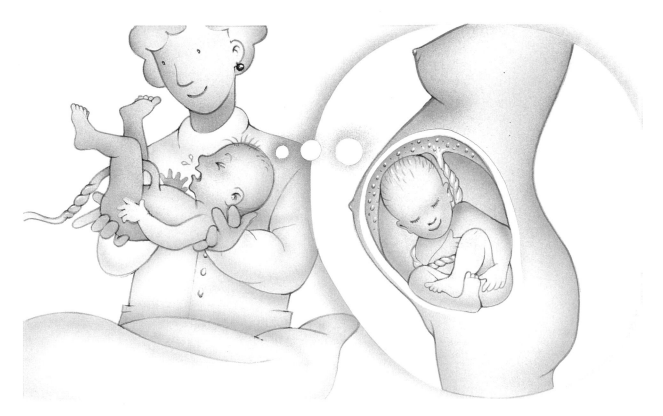

The mother takes her baby into her arms to cuddle and love.

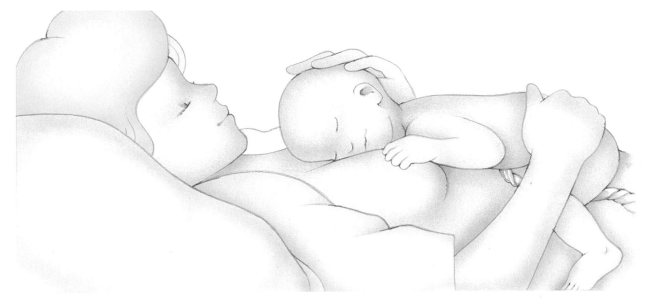

The baby does not need the umbilical cord any more, so the doctor cuts through it. This does not hurt the baby or its mother.

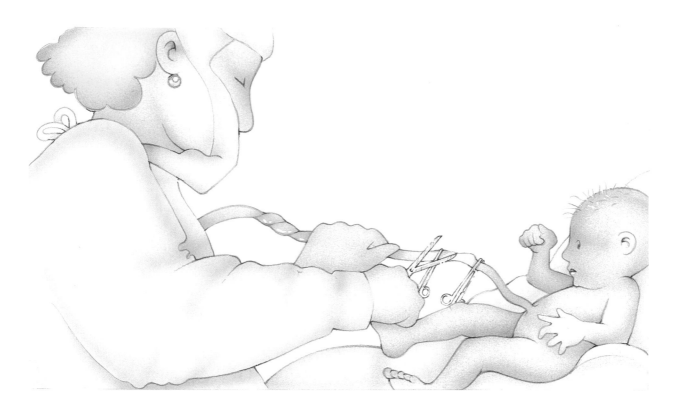

The little bit of cord attached to the baby drops off after two or three days and then the baby has a tummy button.

Finally, the uterus pushes the placenta out through the vagina – it is not needed once the baby is born.

After the birth

Straight after the birth, the baby is given to its mother so they can get to know each other. The mother sometimes cuddles her baby next to her bare skin. This is known as bonding. Some people believe the baby likes to hear the mother's heartbeat.

Then the baby is weighed and measured. A newborn baby usually weighs about three kilos (about 7 lb) and is about 50 cm (19 inches) long.

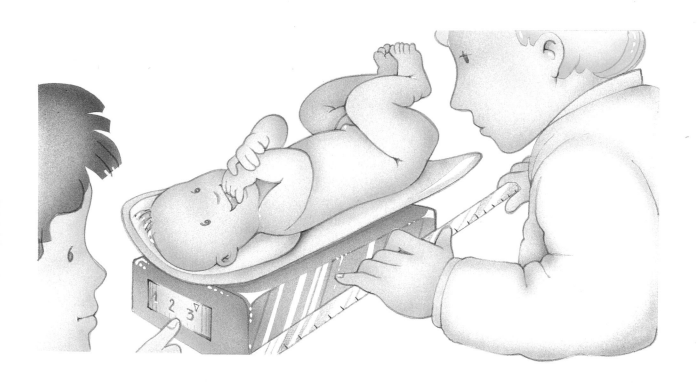

Finally, the baby is dressed and made comfortable so it can sleep in a cot.

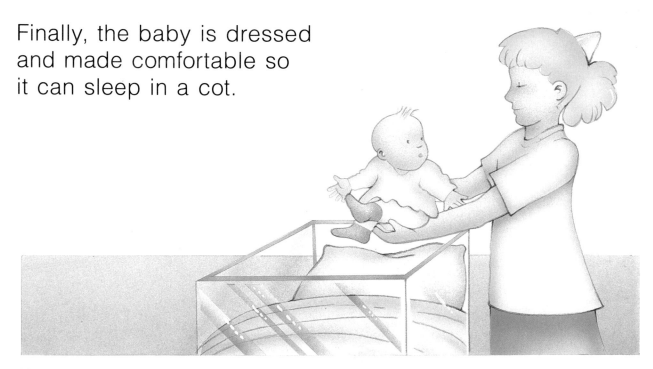

The mother and baby will probably stay in the maternity ward for a few days to rest before going home.

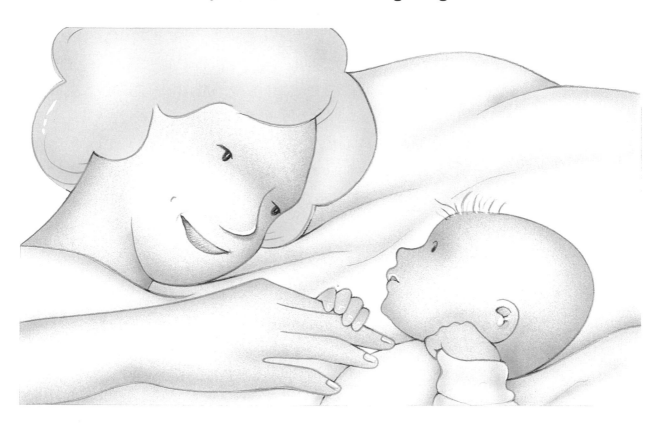

It is a proud and happy moment for the parents when they take their baby home and it becomes part of the family.

What happens when the baby is born too early?

If a baby is born after only seven or eight months in the uterus, it is called a **premature** baby and it is often small and fragile. It is put into a special cot called an **incubator**, which is warm and keeps the baby safe from infection. The baby continues to grow and develop inside the incubator where doctors and nurses can keep an eye on it and check its progress.

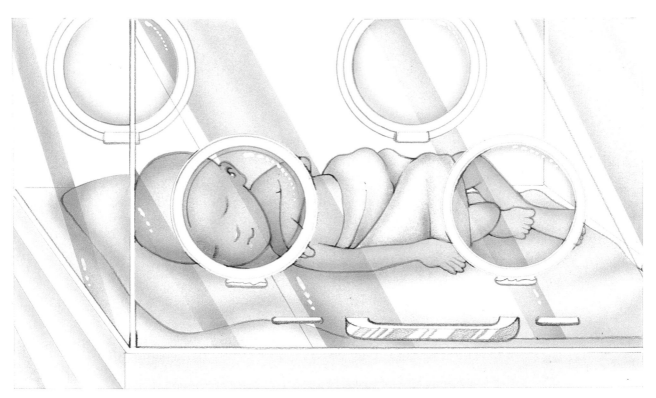

When the mother and father visit their baby, they can touch and stroke it by putting their hands through the holes at the side of the incubator.
After a few weeks, when the baby has gained weight and is strong enough, it can leave the incubator and go home with its mother and father.

Twins

Sometimes an ovary produces two eggs at the same time. If each egg is fertilized by a sperm, two babies will develop. The mother has two babies growing in her uterus. These babies are called **twins**.

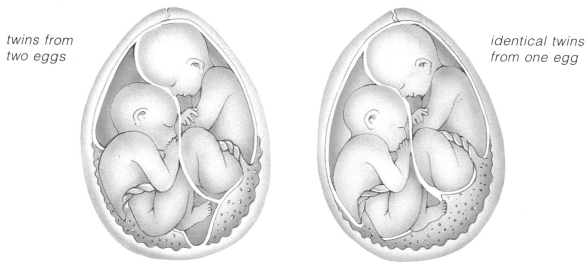

twins from
two eggs

identical twins
from one egg

Occasionally, a fertilized egg splits in two, and two babies are born that look exactly like one another. These babies are called identical twins.

A similar thing happens with triplets, three babies, and quadruplets, four babies.

Baby is hungry

When the baby is hungry, it cries. This is the only way the baby can tell its mother that it needs feeding.
While the mother is pregnant, her breasts get ready to fill with milk so that when the baby is born there will be food for it straight away. When the baby sucks on its mother's breast, milk flows into its mouth.

Some mothers use special baby milk and feed their baby from a bottle – and Dad helps too!

After a couple of months of being fed with a bottle, the baby can eat more solid food. There are lots of different baby foods, with all sorts of flavours to try.

Babies cannot chew food, because they have no teeth, but they can eat cereal and mashed up fruit and vegetables.

At about six months, the baby can hold a rusk and chew on it with its gums. The baby learns to hold a spoon and feed itself. All this time, it is growing bigger and bigger. When a baby is one year old, it can eat most types of food, and can crawl or even walk by itself.

From then on, the baby grows and develops quickly until it is soon a young child.

Glossary of words

The words, which are in bold in the text, are explained below.

amniotic fluid: the liquid that protects the baby inside the uterus.

birth: the moment when the baby leaves the mother's body.

egg: tiny cell produced by the ovary. Also known as an ovule.

Fallopian tubes: narrow tubes that lead from the ovary to the uterus.

female sexual organs: vagina, Fallopian tubes, uterus, ovaries.

fertilization: the moment when a sperm penetrates an egg.

incubator: covered cot which keeps a premature baby safe from infection.

male sexual organs: penis, scrotum, testicles, sperm ducts.

maternity ward: part of a hospital reserved for women about to give birth or who have given birth.

midwife: nurse specially trained to help women give birth.

ovaries: the two female organs that produce eggs.

ovulation: the moment that the egg leaves the ovary.

penis: in an adult, sperm pass along this to enter the woman's vagina. Urine comes out of this when a man or boy goes to the toilet.

placenta: mesh of veins in the lining of the uterus that provide food and oxygen for the developing baby.

premature: a baby born after only seven or eight months in the uterus.

scrotum: the sack of skin that contains the testicles.

semen: liquid containing sperm.

sperm: tiny cell, produced by the testicles, that fertilizes an egg.

sperm duct: thin tube that leads from a testicle to the penis.

testicles: the two male organs that produce sperm.

twins: two babies born at the same time. Either two eggs fertilized by two sperm or one egg fertilized by one sperm that splits into two balls of cells.

umbilical cord: narrow cord that joins the baby to the placenta.

uterus: also called the womb. Female organ in which the baby develops.

vagina: narrow opening between a girl's legs that leads to the uterus.